MW00677254

Published by Barbour Publishing, Inc., P.O. Box 719, Uhrichsville, Ohio 44683
http://www.barbourbooks.com

Member of the
Evangelical Christian
Publishers Association

Printed in China.

WAY TO GO,
Grad!

written and compiled by
Colleen Reece and
Julie Reece-DeMarco

BARBOUR
PUBLISHING, INC.

Congratulations!

You have fought the good fight
You have finished your course.
You have kept the faith.
2 TIMOTHY 4:7 PARAPHRASED

This is your day.

An End and a Beginning. . .

Graduation Day! A time for celebration. Speeches. Diplomas. Hugs and smiles. Gifts from friends and relatives. You can be proud. You have accomplished what you set out to do many years ago.

Graduation Day is also a time for other things: Good-byes to friends with whom you have shared so much. Reflecting on the person you have become and determining who you wish to be in the future. The highway of life stretches out before you. Each curve and crossroad hides unknown joys, sorrows, and challenges.

As you embrace the present and look toward the future, it is your time for celebration, preparation, wisdom, and God. In this special season of your life, may you find that these stories, quotes, Scriptures, and anecdotes help make your journey successful, not just a long, hard road.

To every thing
there is a season,
and a time to every purpose
under the heaven.

ECCLESIASTES 3:1 KJV

A Time For Celebration

This is the day the LORD has made;
let us rejoice and be glad in it.
PSALM 118:24 NIV

Today

Today, whatever may annoy,
The word for me is Joy, just simple Joy.
Whate'er there be of Sorrow
I'll put off till Tomorrow,
And when Tomorrow comes, why then
'Twill be Today and Joy again.

JOHN KENDRICK BANGS (1862-1922)

Seize the Day

An oft-quoted Latin phrase, *carpe diem*, captures the essence of the challenge in each of our lives. To seize the day.

In this age, individuals are bombarded daily with technological advances and a myriad of choices of how to spend each waking minute. TV. Internet. Movies. Reading. Friends. Work. School. Church. Service. All vie for a position of importance on the calendar.

As days and weeks fill with activities, life flies by. It becomes easy to lose the joy of living each moment in the "busyness" of it all. You will never again be in the place you are now. Today is your time of celebration. Stop to enjoy it.

Rejoice evermore.
Pray without ceasing.
In every thing give thanks:
for this is the will of God in Christ Jesus concerning you.
1 THESSALONIANS 5:16–18 KJV

The secret of happiness is not in doing what one likes
but in liking what one has to do.
SIR JAMES MATTHEW BARRIE (1860-1937)

Be content with your surroundings but not with yourself till you have made the most of them.

AUTHOR UNKNOWN

If you ever find happiness by hunting for it,
you will find it as the old woman did her lost spectacles,
safe on her own nose all the time.
JOSH BILLINGS (1818-1885)

Celebrating Shared Experiences

Busy persons often forget the simple joy of being together with family and friends. The humblest meal becomes a celebration when served with love. When you don't think you can stretch the remnants of your food enough to go around, remember what faith can do.

"The people are hungry," the disciples told Jesus. "They have come to hear You, but they have no food."

"There are five thousand men, plus women and children," one reminded Jesus. "What shall we do?"

Simon Peter's brother Andrew shook his head. "There is a lad here who has five barley loaves and two small fishes, but what are they among so many?"

"Make the men sit down," Jesus ordered. He took the boy's lunch, gave thanks, and distributed food to His wondering disciples. They in turn gave it to the people, scarcely believing their eyes when more and more kept coming. When all had eaten, twelve baskets yet remained.

The miracle of the loaves and fishes is one of the most loved Bible stories (paraphrased from John 6:1-14).

A Poignant Memory

Carl Donovan's mother died when he was five. For years, he tried to remember the special dessert she had made for him. All he could recall was that it sparkled and tasted delicious.

At a family get-together shortly after Carl's graduation from college, he mentioned the dessert. To his amazement, his youngest aunt's eyes filled with tears. She said, "Carl, your mom had a tough time after your father died. He left debts she felt obligated to pay. She was too proud to accept help, but she refused to allow life to get her down. She made a game of everything, even her 'special' dessert. It took three steps."

Carl could hardly wait. "What were they?"

"First, Mary lit a candle and set it on the table. Then she sliced an apple or a banana into a shiny, cut glass dish. Finally, she sprinkled sugar over the top. I hope this doesn't spoil your memory."

It didn't. It only increased Carl's love and respect for his mother.

A Tale of Sharing

Remember the wonderful old French folk tale "Stone Soup"? Two strangers came to a hamlet where people were hoarding food for fear of starvation. They persuaded the villagers to bring what they had and put it together in one large kettle. One by one the poor people each brought a small offering:

a carrot or two
a small potato
a handful of beans

The strangers dropped two so-called "magic stones" into the pot, creating "stone soup." The real magic that fed the entire village was not the ordinary rocks the strangers dropped in but the spirit of sharing. . . .

If there's too much month left at the end of your money and your refrigerator is dangerously close to empty, call a few friends. Invite them to bring anything they have on hand and make a luck-of-the-pot celebration. You may end up with a strange menu, but you'll have fun—and something to eat!

Tomorrow

Beyond the shadows of a far distant shore
The promises of tomorrow lie untouched in the mist,
Not quite reality—then again, much more,
Providing the reasons we exist.
    The traces of days left behind grow silent, cease their
        whisperings.
    Only faint memories remind of the joys and sorrows
        life brings.
With gaze ahead and heart behind, we lose the path on
    which we tread,
So intent we are to find the path that lies ahead.
    And when the distant shore is reached,
    When the day draws to a close,
    The mists will lift, and we will see
    The joys of life were the paths we chose.

A Time for Preparation

Choose you this day whom ye will serve. . .
but as for me and my house, we will serve the LORD.
JOSHUA 24:15 KJV

There is no more important time to set your standards for the future than right now. The choices you make today will have tremendous impact on the person you will become. The Boy Scout motto prompts its members to "Be Prepared." Likewise, as we look toward tomorrow there is no wiser counsel we can heed. Each decision, each action we take, affects our course in life.

Those who have camped know wandering even one degree off the mark on a compass can result in being miles off the final destination. Stepping out in a direction in life without a compass can have the same result.

No one understands this principle better than Mark. Sitting in his drug rehabilitation counselor's office, friendless, penniless, and homeless, thirty-one-year-old Mark struggled for answers.

"I don't understand," he questioned Dale, his counselor. "I had it all. Prom king, high school football star, college scholarship, great girlfriend. How could I lose it overnight?"

Dale's answer came back quietly. "When did you make your *first* bad decision?"

Step by step Mark reviewed each small move off course he had made—skipping class here, attending a questionable party there, hanging out with friends who didn't share his standards, trying something "just once," choosing not to study, not finding time for parents, not finding time for God.

As the list grew, Mark realized each small decision had formed the basis for a habit that now plagued him. "Boy," he mused. "I wish I could have a couple of those decisions back."

Decide today who you will be, and tomorrow, you'll be glad.

Always Remember

- Six months after graduation, a good reputation will get you farther than anything on your resume.

- "I'm sorry" and "I blew it" make more friends than any explanation.

- Always write down the name (first and last), position, telephone number, date, and time you talk with someone. Keep it in a file.

- Buy a calendar at the beginning of the year. Write in important birthdays, anniversaries, and holidays. Make a note a week before each to send a card.

- Every year on Mother's or Father's Day, Valentine's Day, Christmas, or on your birthday, take time to write cards and tell people how much they mean to you. Once a month, write a letter to someone who has changed your life for the better.

There is no one you will ever meet who cannot do something better or see something more clearly than you can. Ask yourself every time you meet someone new, "What can I learn from this person?"

According to Henry Wadsworth Longfellow, youth comes but once in a lifetime. Perhaps, but it remains strong in many for their entire lives.

Recycle and treat the earth with respect. It may be the only legacy you leave to future generations.

Spend more time with friends and family. You will never regret it.

Start every day by giving your Heavenly Father a "Thank You" for simply being alive.

There is always Someone who understands exactly how we feel.

Jesus walked every path, felt every feeling, and overcame every obstacle we will ever have to face.

I Have Choices. . .
but what are they?

*Love your enemies and
pray for those who persecute you.*
MATTHEW 5:44 NIV

Learning to get along with others is the hardest job any of us face. Our futures depend on the degree to which we develop our people skills now. In every case, we have choices. Just ask Brian.

Brian couldn't look at his roommate without gritting his teeth. Aaron's habits and comments ranged from annoying to totally offensive. If Brian had to sit through one more meal watching Aaron chew his dinner with an open mouth or explain to one more date that the dirty socks and dishes in the living room weren't his, he was going to strangle his roommate.

One day a sentence from something Brian read stuck in his mind. *If you serve someone, it will change your own attitude.* "The person who wrote that didn't have to smell Aaron's socks," he muttered. "But if I don't do something, I'll go nuts. I guess it can't do any harm. Besides, what choice do I have?"

Brian found a card, scribbled, "Hope you do well on your test," pinned it to Aaron's pillow (which he found in the midst of his roommate's dirty-clothes pile) and left for class.

Later that day, Brian returned to the empty apartment. A plate of chocolate chip cookies and a "thinking of you" card lay on his bed.

Change came. Not so much in Aaron—although he did grow more pleasant and made an effort to keep the apartment livable— but mostly in Brian's perception.

Several years later, he received a card from the roommate who had almost driven him crazy. It spoke of how important Brian's friendship was to Aaron and how much it had touched his life. The note ended, *"You touched my life in more ways than you will ever know. I just want to say, you would be proud of what I am today."*

Brian stared at the message, thankful that he didn't miss knowing Aaron simply because of his dirty socks *and* Brian's unwillingness to look for the good in his roommate.

Don't Slam Doors Behind You

Jack breathed a sigh of relief on the last day of the part-time job he had held to help pay his way through college. His brand-new degree meant the opportunity for a more prestigious, higher paying position.

"Don't forget," Jack's supervisor said. "We can always use you."

No way will I be back, Jack thought. He didn't want to be rude, so he just smiled—one of the wisest decisions of his life. He discovered after graduation that jobs were scarce in his chosen field, and the bills kept coming in. Part-time work at his former place of employment brought in a small, but steady paycheck until Jack found a job where he could better use his education and experience.

A Time for Wisdom

Trust in the LORD with all thine heart;
and lean not unto thine own understanding.
In all thy ways acknowledge him,
and he shall direct thy paths.
PROVERBS 3:5-6 KJV

Mahatma Gandhi said, "It is unwise to be too sure of one's own wisdom. It is healthy to be reminded that the strongest might weaken and the wisest might err."

Life and Learning

Life is about learning. Opportunities for learning are everywhere. Wisdom can be derived from observation, conversation, study, or experience. Watching and emulating those individuals who have characteristics you would like to exemplify helps facilitate personal growth. Speaking with others who have made mistakes helps us avoid repeating them. Studying, pondering, and praying about problems often results in enlightenment. While all these methods are helpful, experience is often the best teacher.

One of the few guarantees in life is that it will not be easy. Each person's life will be touched with hardship and trial. The lessons learned in these difficult times, however, are often the most beautiful and poignant.

Alicia pulled the covers over her head and shut her eyes against the sun shining through the window. Another day she couldn't find the energy to face. After her father's sudden death the month before, Alicia found life just didn't seem worth living. Thinking of her beloved dad started the tears afresh. The sleeping pills on her bedside table looked awfully tempting.

Her dismal thoughts were interrupted by a knock on the door.

Brent, her ever-optimistic pastor, came in. "Alicia, we need to talk."

"I don't have anything to say to you. You couldn't possibly understand," Alicia muttered.

"Well," her pastor explained. "I hit a really rough period in my life. My parents were killed in a freak car accident. Within a few years, my wife was stricken with cancer, and I was left a single father of a young family. I lost my job that same week. I wasn't sure how I would go on."

"I don't understand," Alicia questioned. "You are always so happy!"

Brent smiled. "At first I just forced myself to get up each day. Soon I found the Lord was bringing me into contact with others whose stories were as sad as mine. I truly understood their pain. It was as if my heart were filling with love and compassion each time I helped others.

"One person I met became my best friend. One, who had lost her husband suddenly, later became my wife. My life is richer now because of my experiences."

Alicia looked toward the sun shining in her window. Maybe there was a little light in even the darkest day.

Road Map

Self-evaluation can help you find out where you are going and how to get there. Answer the questions as frankly as you can. Go back in six months or a year and do the questions again. Compare the answers to see how you're doing.

1. Who am I?
   Who do I want to become?
   Why?
2. What are the five most important things in my life today?
   Why?
3. What do I believe will be the most important things in my life?
   Why?
4. Where do I see myself in five, twenty, fifty years?
   How will I achieve these goals?
5. How am I making the world a better place right now?
   How will I make it a better place in the future?
   When and how will I start?

Viewpoints

In his wonderful book *Man's Search for Meaning*, Viktor Frankl tells the story of Dr. J., scourge of one of the worst German death camps during World War II. Never had a man so evil walked the halls of horror. Whispers of his inhuman experiments floated through the camp, and strong men shuddered like frightened children.

Years later a man came to Viktor Frankl's study. The conversation turned to Germany, the war, and the concentration camps. "Did you know Dr. J.?" the visitor asked.

Frankl nodded.

The other's face lighted. "We were in prison together. He showed himself to be the best comrade you can imagine! He gave consolation to everybody. He lived up to the highest conceivable moral standard. He was the best friend I ever met during my long years in prison!"

The incident caused Viktor Frankl to write words that reflect the depths of God's mercy: "Every human being has the freedom to change at any instant."

Man looks at the outward appearance,
but the LORD looks at the heart.

1 SAMUEL 16:7 NIV

The Other Side of the Picture

A professor who often served on negotiating teams told his college students, "No matter how impossible it seems, each of us has something in common with every other human being." When the disbelieving stares of his students showed they didn't agree, he told this story:

His most difficult experience came when he was part of a team involved in negotiating with a member of a white supremacy group. An African-American, the professor vainly tried to put aside his discomfort and find a common meeting ground—anything from which to start. He failed. Throughout the luncheon meeting, the professor met only with resistance. An hour later, negotiations remained at an impasse.

The professor took out his wallet to pay the bill. The supremacist glimpsed a picture. "Are those your children?" he asked.

A hundred questions raced through the professor's mind. If he said yes, would it mean endangering his family? He hesitated, but reluctantly nodded.

"These are my children," the other replied. He brought out his wallet and proudly showed pictures. The single thing they had in common provided a strong enough meeting for them to complete a successful negotiation.

Not in My Album!

Although challenged by her professor's assertion and story, Lindsay felt exceptions to the rule existed; namely, Mark. He sought her out at every opportunity, bombarding her with his own beliefs. "You don't belong in college," he maintained. "No woman does. Women should be in the home instead of taking places men should have."

After a few attempts to defend herself, Lindsay simply avoided Mark whenever she could. She decided he was the biggest jerk she had ever encountered. In spite of this, she couldn't forget what her professor had said. One day she made an effort to talk with Mark on a neutral subject. When he responded appropriately, she tried another. To her amazement, she discovered they did have things in common. Not a lot, but enough to prove the professor's point—each person does have something in common with everyone else.

29

A Time for God

*But seek ye first the kingdom of God,
and his righteousness.*
MATTHEW 6:33 KJV

Given the time-consuming activities of our daily lives, finding time
for God is often neglected. He is relegated to the back burner where
He sits until another major crisis arises, and He is remembered.

That is the hard way. God has promised to be with His children
every moment of every day—if we will let Him.

No Olympic athlete would consider telling his or her personal
trainer, "Don't bother showing up for my practice sessions the next
few months. I'll call you if I think I need you." That would be a sure
recipe for failure.

Trainers are there to spot problems, develop programs, and fine-
tune exercises to meet the needs of their trainees on a day-by-day

basis. It is that level of attention, that external, impartial eye, that ensures outstanding performance.

Likewise, we need the constant scrutiny and assistance, the daily encouragement, and attention from our Heavenly Father to ensure that we turn in a gold-medal performance in this life.

I will lift up mine eyes unto the hills,
from whence cometh my help.
My help cometh from the LORD,
which made heaven and earth.
PSALM 121:1-2 KJV

Alone

Be still, and know that I am God.
PSALM 46:10 KJV

One of the lowest times Renee ever experienced came just after she began her first year of graduate school. She had to leave for college several states away the morning after her grandmother's memorial service. She missed her an awful lot. Grandma was a friend who believed in Renee, listened, and understood.

One evening, Renee dragged home from classes. She looked at the stars, wishing Grandma was there with her. Being the youngest member of her class meant competing with those much older and more experienced. How could she concentrate on increasingly difficult studies when she felt so alone and sad?

Renee thought of her grandma's memorial service and the friends and family who had been there. Her mind focused on Marian, a victim of several disabling illnesses.

Marian arrived in a wheelchair. She had spent hours during the final, hard days with Renee's aunt who lived with and cared for Grandma. After the service, Renee and her sister talked with Marian.

She told them, "Right now everyone is giving your aunt the support she needs: flowers, cards, time. I'm going to wait and watch these next few months. There will be times when she will need love and support and won't be able to let people know how much she is hurting. I'll give my flowers then."

How nice it would be to have someone like Marian right now, Renee thought. *Someone watching to make sure I'm okay; ready to lend a listening ear; able to recognize things aren't all right without my having to say anything.*

Through her dark thoughts, Renee felt a small light. She already had Someone. He had been with her all along. He knew when things were the darkest in her life, without her having to say a word. He knew when she needed a flower, a card, or a listening ear. Renee realized no matter how far away she was from her family, no matter how hard, discouraging, or lonely the road she walked, He would always be there for her.

Jesus is also called Emmanuel—*God with us.* Hundreds of years ago Moses told the people, *"The Lord. . .will be with you; He will never leave you nor forsake you"* (Deuteronomy 31:8 NIV). It's just as true now as it was then.

The 23rd Psalm (KJV)

The LORD is my shepherd; I shall not want.
He maketh me to lie down in green pastures:
he leadeth me beside the still waters.
He restoreth my soul:
he leadeth me in the paths of righteousness
for his name's sake.
Yea, though I walk through the valley of the shadow
of death, I will fear no evil: for thou art with me;
thy rod and thy staff they comfort me.
Thou preparest a table before me
in the presence of mine enemies:
thou anointest my head with oil; my cup runneth over.
Surely goodness and mercy shall follow me
all the days of my life:
and I will dwell in the house of the LORD for ever.

Taking Time

Many years ago a woman lived with her sister and brother in a spacious home. She loved to entertain, although company meant long hours of preparation. Anything less than perfection in housekeeping, food, or service would not be tolerated by the mistress of the home.

One particular day, the woman was especially tired from all the necessary preparations. To make matters worse, she found her sister intently listening to their visitor instead of helping with the serving.

"Don't you care that my sister has left all the work to me?" the weary woman demanded of their special visitor. "Tell her she should get up and help."

Jesus looked at the frustrated woman and quietly said, "Martha, Martha, you are careful and troubled about many things, but one thing is needed. Your sister Mary has chosen the better part. It will not be taken from her" (paraphrased from Luke 10:41).

Some believe Jesus chastised Martha for being conscientious. He actually praised her for attending to duty. Then he pointed out Mary's choice to listen to His teachings was the better choice and something Martha needed.

Making good choices is important. Making those God considers better is vital.

The Race

An unknown author tells the story of a race. Trembling with fear, hope, and excitement, young children line up. Their parents watch from the sidelines, cheering for their kids.

The whistle blows and off they go! A boy near the lead thinks how proud his dad must be.

The next moment, he slips and falls.

"Quit! Give up; you're beaten!" the crowd jeers.

For a moment, he believes it. Then the fallen boy sees his father's face. He can almost hear his dad shout, "Get up and win the race!"

He leaps to his feet and races on, only to fall a second time. A third! Three strikes and you're out. Why go on? Yet his father's voice rings in his ears.

"Get up and win the race!"

The boy springs to his feet. He cannot win, but he will not quit. He hears the cheers for the winner and keeps on running. Head bowed, he comes in last, to louder cheers than the winner received.

"I didn't do well," he sadly tells his father.

His wonderful dad says, "To me you won. Each time you fell, you rose."

The boy becomes a man. He faces dark, hard times. Always the memory of the little boy he once was helps him know all you have to do to win is to keep on getting up and going on.

"Quit! Give up; you're beaten," people still shout in his face.

But his father's voice rings in his ears, "Get up and win the race!"

FROM: The Apsotle Paul
TO: Timothy, (whom Paul called his dear son):

I have fought the good fight,
I have finished the race,
I have kept the faith.
Now there is in store for me the crown of righteousness,
which the Lord, the righteous Judge,
will award to me on that day.
2 TIMOTHY 4:7–8 NIV

37

What?

Several years ago a pastor shocked his congregation by saying, "I don't want to be a follower of Jesus."

When the ripple of indignation sweeping through the church subsided, the pastor explained. "Followers forever trail along behind. I don't want to spend my life *behind* Jesus. I want to walk *beside* Him; to be His companion and friend. . . ."

Jesus wants to be our Companion, Friend, and Helper. The psalmist David writes, *God is our refuge and strength, an ever present help in trouble* (Psalm 46:1, NIV). Countless inspiring stories are told of persons trapped in dangerous situations who discover God's "ever present help" when they cry out to Him. Many gratefully share how inner peace replaced their panic. Children rescued from unspeakable conditions have told reporters, "I was really scared. Then I remembered Jesus loves me and would be with me until someone came."

Making a Way

I will even make a way in the wilderness.
Isaiah 43:19 KJV

Eddie Rickenbacker (1890-1973), the United States' leading World War I air ace and later president and chairman of the board of directors of Eastern Airlines, was one of many recipients of God's mercy.

Rickenbacker and seven companions were forced down into the Pacific Ocean during World War II. For twenty-four days and nights they drifted. Hopes for rescue sank lower with each setting sun.

Only God knows how many prayers for help ascended during their eternity of waiting or how many prayers of thankfulness followed when help came.

You may never be adrift on a wide, stormy ocean or hopelessly lost in a wilderness. Yet the road of life winds through perilous ravines and over forbidding mountains, as well as through sunny valleys. You have a choice: Face and triumph over life's obstacles, or merely survive. Deciding to walk beside God and learning to be His companion *now*—before the way grows rough, steep, and filled with crises—will make the difference.

Final Choice

Helen Keller called life,
"Either a daring experience or nothing at all."

Which will yours be?